Christ Optimizes Victory in Desolation
Prayers for Uncertain Times
Carol J. Williams

© April 2020 by Carol J. Williams

All rights reserved worldwide. This book is protected by the copyright laws of the United States of America.

No part of this publication may be reproduced, distributed, or transmitted in any form or by any means, including photocopying, recording, or other electronic or mechanical methods, without the prior written permission of the publisher, except in the case of brief quotations embodied in critical reviews and certain other non-commercial uses permitted by copyright law. For permission requests, write to the publisher, addressed "Attention: Permissions Coordinator," at the address below.

Published by Pecan Tree Publishing
April 2020
Hollywood, FL
www.pecantreebooks.com
adminservices@pecantreebooks.com

978-1-7347430-2-9 Paperback
978-1-7347430-3-6 Ebook
Library of Congress Control Number: 2020907824

Cover and Interior Design by: Charlyn Samson

Pecan Tree Publishing

www.pecantreebooks.com

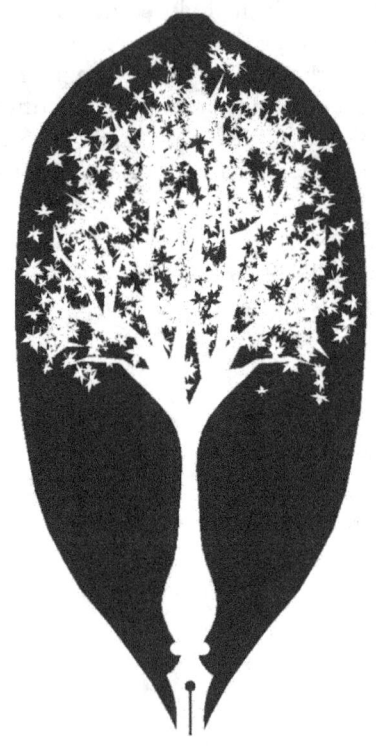

New Voices | New Styles | New Vision –
Creating a New Legacy of Dynamic Authors and Titles
Hollywood, FL

CONTENTS

Repentance 1

Thanksgiving 7

Restoration 14

Salvation 21

Healing 27

Wealth 33

Fear 38

Faith 43

Peace 48

Hope 53

Strength 58

Love 63

Humility 70

Grief 75

Christ Optimizes Victory in Desolation

PRAYERS FOR UNCERTAIN TIMES

Carol J. Williams

PREFACE

Men should always pray and faint not! Yes, in the midst of a global pandemic, we should pray! The prayers of the righteous availeth much! God does hear and answers prayers. Yes, He does!

I am honored the Lord trusts me to stand in the gap for individuals. C(hrist) O(optimizes) V(ictory) I(n) D(esolation) was birthed out of prayer a week prior to this writing. I heard the Lord say, "write a book of prayers for the Body of Christ related to COVID-19."

These prayers during a season of uncertainty remind the Body of Christ that God is with us, Optimizing His Victory in Desolation. As He is optimizing His Victory in Desolation, we too must optimize His victory in the midst of this onslaught of a deadly virus, understanding we always win.

A special thanks to my Pastors Joseph & LaQuisha Brown who have taught me the importance of prayer and how to pray strategically. I am appreciative of leaders of prayer.

REPENTANCE

When we Hear the word REPENTANCE or REPENT, we often think it simply means saying, "I am sorry." Repentance is more than that. Repentance means to make a turn or change in direction. Repentance shows God's unconditional love because He knows we are going to come back and ask forgiveness – again - for the same thing.

Repentance frees us from being prideful. It allows us to be honest with God so that we're able to tell Him the truth about ourselves. It reminds us that we all have sinned and come short of the glory of God.

Repentance requires opening our mouths and confessing things not pleasing to God. God already knows we've done those things; He just wants to hear us confess them so we can be forgiven and receive His forgiveness.

What I love about the Lord is once we ask Him to forgive us; He is faithful and just to forgive all our sins. The Lord is not only faithful and just to forgive us, but He doesn't remember our sins! Thank you, Jesus! Men remember our sins, but Jesus forgives them!

REPENTANCE

You're God and besides You there's no other God. There's no God who compares to You! You're King of kings and Lord of lords.

We start by asking You to create within us a clean heart and renew a right spirit within us. (Psalm 51:10 KJV) We thank you for Your Word that washes us. (Ephesians 5:26 KJV) We ask You to forgive us for those things we know displease You. We ask You to forgive us for the things we've done that we didn't know displeased You. We apologize!

Father, please forgive us for placing other gods before You! Yes, please forgive us for allowing the coronavirus to be greater in our world than You. We apologize for magnifying it over You. We understand and recognize You're a jealous God and will have no other gods before You. (Exodus 34:14 KJV) We tear down every god that we've exalted. We dethrone them now and place You back on the Throne. Father, You reign.

Father, forgive us for not drawing close to You in the midst

of the storm. We apologize for running from You instead of running to You. Lord, draw us back to Your bleeding side. We quickly run back to Your presence where even during COVID-19 we can experience the fullness of joy knowing that at Your right hand, there are pleasures forevermore. (Psalm 16:11 KJV) Lord, give us a desire to hunger and thirst after righteousness knowing that we will be filled. (Matthew 5:6 KJV) We want to be filled with more of You and less of ourselves. We want more of You!

Father, forgive us for being disobedient to Your will, way, and purpose for our lives. Lord, we want You, Your will, way, and purpose for our lives. Your will be done! (Matthew 6:10 KJV) We submit our will, way, and purpose to Yours. We relinquish our control for Your complete control.

Father, forgive us for not totally trusting You. We will trust in You with all our hearts, and not lean to our own understanding, and in all our ways we will acknowledge You knowing that You're going to direct our paths. (Proverbs 3:6) We trust You to see us through times of uncertainty. We trust You with our lives as we know that our times are in Your hands. (Psalm 31:15) We trust You with our lives because You're the giver of life. We trust You knowing that You're not a man that You should lie nor the son of man that You need to repent. (Numbers 23:19 KJV) You're the God that always makes good on Your promises and this virus, nor any other, won't stop the manifestations of Your promises in our lives.

We trust You again!

Father, forgive us for allowing our moments of anger towards You to paralyze our relationship with You. We will move forward towards Your will and purpose for our lives. We will find the strength to rely on Your ability in this season to be quick to hear, slow to speak, and slow to anger. (James 1:19 KJV)

As we close, we don't just read and articulate these words; we make a conscious decision to turn from all those things that don't bring You glory and honor! We repent and turn to You so our sins may be wiped out, that the times of refreshing may come from You. (Acts 3:19) Thank you for giving us another chance to make things right and experience the fullness of who You are.

My Prayer, Thoughts or Revelation

THANKSGIVING

When we see the word THANKSGIVING, most of us think of the holiday. While Thanksgiving is a holiday, let's consider it from the spiritual side. THANKSGIVING, is about being grateful or having a grateful heart. In ALL THINGS, we should give thanks.

We don't want to be like the 10 lepers in the Bible who were healed by Jesus. Jesus healed 10 but only one returned to say, "thank you!" Lord, we pause to tell You - thank you!

I know it doesn't make sense, but we should give thanks in everything. Yes, in everything we can find something to be thankful for. You may be thinking, "Carol, do you see what's going on with COVID-19?" Yes, I do see. The ability to see is something to be thankful for. "Carol, do you hear what's going on in the news?" Yes, I do hear. The ability to hear is something to be thankful for.

It's amazing how we have a greater appreciation for lyrics. Perhaps then, the song "Thank You" by Walter Hawkins song quite often still and recorded more than 30 years ago, will drive this point home. "Tragedies are commonplace. All kinds of diseases, people are slipping away. Economics down, people can't get enough pay but as for me all I can say is, thank you Lord for all you've done for me."

There are times when we should pray a prayer of thanksgiving. Yes, just giving God thanks and not asking Him for anything. Giving Him thanks not only for the things He's done but for who He is!

Lord, we thank you!

THANKSGIVING

Thank you, Lord, yes even during the difficult discomfort of this thing called COVID-19. You've been good and Your mercy endures forever. The mere fact we're able to read and articulate this prayer is a great indication that You're good. We thank you for the small things. We thank you for the ability to see. We thank you for the ability to open our mouths to pray and give You thanks.

Thank you that even now, in one of the worst pandemics the world has seen You're keeping our minds. You said in Your Word, if we keep our minds on You that You would keep us in perfect peace. We thank you for keeping our minds. We thank you that we know our names. We thank you that our minds are sound. We thank you that we are transformed by the renewing of our minds. (Romans 12:2 KJV) We thank you that we have Your mind! (I Cor 2:16 KJV) Thank you because our minds are renewed and our thoughts are renewed. Yes, we're thinking on things that are true, honest, just, pure, lovely, and of a good report. (Philippians 4:8 KJV). We give You thanks!

Thank you, Jehovah Rapha, (the Lord that heals). We thank you that we're healed from all manner of sickness and diseases. (Matthew 4:23) Thank you for taking stripes for our healing!

(Isaiah 53:5 KJV) Thank you that healing is our bread! (Matthew 15:26). We thank you that we're in good health even as our soul prospers. (3 John 1:2) Thank you that as healing is in Your wings, You're flapping Your wings of healing over us. (Malachi 4:2 KJV). Thank you that health is restored unto us and our wounds are healed. (Jeremiah 30:17 KJV) Thank you for mending the broken heart. (Psalm 147:3 KJV) Even when we don't feel healed, we're healed, and we give You thanks.

Thank you for Your mercy! Lord, You didn't give us what we deserved but You had mercy on us! It's because of Your mercies that we're not consumed, because Your compassions fail not. They are new every morning; great is thy faithfulness. Thank you for Your faithfulness.

We've not always been consistent and faithful towards You. We thank you for being consistent and faithful in our world. You're a faithful God. You love us unconditionally. We thank you for Your faithfulness that endures to all generations. (Psalm 119:90 KJV)

It was Your love that lifted us out of dark places. We thank you for Your love! Thank you, Jesus, for being our greatest example of love. You laid down Your life for us. Thank you for such a love that allows us to have abundant life.

Lord, all we need, You are! You're Jehovah Jireh, the Lord will provide. We thank you for supplying all our needs according to Your riches in glory by Christ Jesus. We thank you even when it looks like lack abounds; there is no lack because You're our Shepherd and we shall not want. (Psalm 23:1 KJV) Thank you that there's no good thing You withhold from us providing we walk up right. (Psalm 84:11) Thank you Lord for Your daily provision.

Thank you for being the best illuminator. You're the light of our world. (John 8:12 KJV) You're the light of our salvation, whom shall we fear. (Psalm 27:1 KJV) You're the God who enlightens our darkness. (Psalm 18:28 KJV) We thank you that as long as we have You, we will always have light.

We thank you and give You great praise because You've done it again! (Psalm 52:9 KJV)

My Prayer, Thoughts or Revelation

PRAYERS FOR UNCERTAIN TIMES

RESTORATION

God will and can restore! RESTORE means to make like new! We are living witnesses that God can restore! Take a moment and reflect over your life. I know you may not be 100% the person you want to be; however, you're not the same person you used to be. If you don't feel this statement applies to you, make the confession of God's Word, "I am in Christ therefore I am a new creature, old things passed away; behold all things are become new." (2 Corinthians 5: 17 KJV)

Restore: to bring back into existence or re-establish. God is going to bring things back into existence after this. Yes, He is going to restore. In some cases, things are going to be better than their previous state.

Declaring restoration in desolation requires faith. Let's believe God despite desolation, and decree and declare God's Word. Lord, You, who have shown us great and sore troubles, shalt quicken us again, and shalt bring us up again from the depths of the earth. Thou shalt increase our greatness and comfort us on every side.

COVID-19 appears to be eating up some things in our lives. There's still restoration and God will restore unto us the years that the locust hath eaten, the cankerworm, the caterpillar, and the palmerworm. (Joel 2:25 KJV)

RESTORATION

Father, there's been many losses as it relates to the coronavirus. We decree and declare that You're restoring our faith in You! We admit that we have allowed the tragedy of this virus to weaken our faith. Lord, we pray as You've prayed for us that our faith fail not. We have faith to believe You again. We realize that faith is the substance of things hoped for and the evidence of things not seen. (Hebrews 11:1 KJV) We can't see how things are going to work out with our natural eyes, but we believe You! We make a conscious decision to walk by faith not by sight. (2 Corinthians 5:7 KJV) We have complete faith in You. We understand without faith it's impossible to please You! (Hebrews 11:6 KJV) It's our desire to please You so thank you for our faith being restored.

Father, we thank you that our focus is being restored. Yes, COVID-19 has been our focus and not You. We can begin to see clearly in death, change and despair, the great and mighty things that You are still doing. Yes, You, still are doing great and mighty things. Yes, You, are. Our focus has been so off that we could not see You because so many are dying. You're canceling death. You're healing people from this virus. You still are a miraculous God! Lord, we thank you as our focus changes, our thoughts will change to really think on things that are lovely, just pure, and of good report. Thank you for restoration of focus!

Father we thank you that our finances are being restored. We call on Jehovah Jireh; the Lord will provide. Thank you for making ways out of no way. We decree and declare that men are going to give unto our bosom; good measure, pressed down shaken together, and running over. (Luke 6:38 KJV) We call forth money! We call forth jobs. We call forth grants. We call forth scholarships. We will not lack in this season. You're our Shepherd and we shall not lack anything. (Psalm 23: 1 KJV) The earth is the Lord's, and the fullness thereof and they that dwell therein. (Psalm 24:1 KJV) We decree a river of finances even in what looks like a desert. Thank you, Jesus. We have increase! Thank you for increase. The wealth of the wicked is laid up for us and in this season, it's being released to our hands. Lord even now as we're praying, we cup our hands to receive money! Thank you, Jesus!

Father, we thank you that You're restoring our health. Yes, You're the God that can and will restore health. You're the God that heals all manner of sickness and diseases. Jesus by Your stripes we're already healed. Our healing is being restored in our spirit, body, and soul. Yes, we're healed. It's Your desire that we be in good health even as our soul prospers. (3 John 1:2 KJV) Yes, those who are infected with COVID-19 are healed and there will be no residue of the virus. They are completely healed. We thank you for the power of Your blood. We plead the blood over our bodies from the crown of our head to the soles of our feet even as healing is manifesting. Lord, heal! You are an able God! You are a miraculous God! You are restoring our health. We celebrate complete healing!

Father, we decree and declare that our strength is restored. We are strengthened. The joy of the Lord is our strength! (Nehemiah

8:10) We have strength. Your Word says let the weak say, I am strong! (Joel 3:19 KJV) We are strong! Yes, we are! It's You who giveth power to the faint and to those that hath no might; You increase their strength. (Isaiah 40: 29 KJV) Strengthen us Lord! Strengthen us Lord! We not only seek Your face but seek Your strength.

(I Chronicles 16:11 KJV).

My Prayer, Thoughts or Revelation

SALVATION

SALVATION means to deliver or rescue from sin. Jesus want's everyone to experience His gift of salvation. Individuals can only experience Jesus' gift of salvation from us offering them the gift we have already received.

It's imperative we make a conscious decision during COVID-19 to increase our witness of Jesus and offer salvation to those who have not accepted Him as their personal Savior. We want to make sure that individuals know where they will spend eternity. It's imperative we present the simplicity of salvation.

This is the time to tell of Jesus' love for the world. It's because Jesus lives that they and we can live also. It's time to tell them that Jesus is not about condemnation but love.

Jesus saves! Yes, Jesus delivers and rescues.

SALVATION

Father as individuals are dying rapidly from the coronavirus strain known as COVID-19, we pray that You would save those individuals who don't' know You in the pardon of their sins. God, You so loved the world that You gave Your only begotten son that whosoever believeth in Him should not perish but have everlasting life. (John 3:16) It's not Your desire or plan that anyone should die and go to hell. As we pray for salvation, we recognize that there's no other name under heaven given among men, whereby we must be saved. (Acts 4:12). It's at the name of Jesus every knee shall bow and every tongue shall confess that You are God. (Romans 14:11).

Father we pray for the individuals who don't feel they are worth Your love. Please cause them to know their worth. You loved us so much that You decided to give Your best (Jesus) so we could live. Lord, cause them to know You loved them so much that You sought them out and desire to save them. (Luke 19:10) Please cause them to know that You didn't send Jesus into the world to condemn but that through Him they might be saved. (John 3:17) Father, show them that You're not condemning them but loving them. We ask that You help them understand that You're not like man. When You make promises to love them, You keep that promise.

Save Jesus! Save Jesus! We pray for the individuals who think accepting Jesus as their personal Savior is hard and complex. Lord, I pray they would begin to confess You as Jesus, The Christ, with their mouths and believe in their hearts that God raised You from the dead so that they shall be saved. (Romans 10:9) You are a God that can save!

Father, as they accept You as their personal Savior, cause them to understand it doesn't mean things will be easy but that there's a greater assurance that You're always with them. We pray that along with accepting You as their personal Savior they develop an intimate relationship with You.

We pray individuals find a church home that teaches the truth of Your Word. We pray as they attend church faithfully You would begin to give them a desire for more of You. We pray that You would fill them with You. Lord we thank you that they will not walk in religion but relationship!

We thank you for saving souls! Thank you for Your gift of salvation!

Please help us as the Body of Christ to offer Your gift of salvation to all those we come in contact with.

Perhaps you read this prayer and you've never accepted Jesus as your personal Savior. It's simple as repeating this prayer: Lord, I confess that I am a sinner and I want Your gift of Salvation. I believe Jesus Christ died on the cross for my sins. I believe Jesus was buried and rose from the grave for me. I accept Jesus into my heart and believe that He has saved me. Thank you, Jesus, for saving me!

You are now saved! Welcome to God's Kingdom!

Salvation is not about a feeling. Salvation is about knowing you have accepted Jesus into your heart and believing in His death, burial, and resurrection!

My Prayer, Thoughts or Revelation

HEALING

HEALING, is to be free from disease. God is a Healer! God is a Healer! God is a Healer! God can Heal from coronavirus and all ailments.

We are unable to determine how God chooses to Heal. My best friend died from breast cancer. Her favorite scripture was, "I shall not die, but live and declare the works of the LORD." (Psalm 118:17) I admit when she died, I was upset with God. I couldn't wrap my mind around her quoting this passage and then dying. I will never forget what her pastor said during the eulogy, "She is healed. She has a new body." In that moment the words were not helping because I wanted her here. I came to accept that she had in fact been healed. God can heal miraculously, use medicine or doctors, or whatever He chooses. It's imperative not to focus on the method but on the healer!

COVID-19 looks like death; and in some eyes it may look like there will never be a cure. God sees it differently. God gave His son, Jesus who took stripes for our healing. Healing is our portion! This virus is not until death! We are going to live and not die!

HEALING

We start this prayer by calling on Jehovah Rophe (The Lord who heals). Jesus heal us! We recognize we need Your healing. You're our Great Physician and there's nothing too hard for You. COVID-19 is not too hard for You. Lord, You're our healer. Heal now, Jesus!

We pray that You would heal our land. You said in Your Word "if my people, which are called by name, shall humble themselves, and pray, and seek my face, and, turn from our wicked ways; then You will hear from heaven, and forgive our sins, and will heal our land." (2 Chronicles 7:14) Lord, help us do the pre-requisites so our land can be healed. Lord, cause us to humble ourselves, pray, seek Your face, and turn from our wicked ways. We ask You to forgive us for our disobedience that could be a stumbling block to You healing the land. We believe You're going to heal our land.

We pray that You heal our bodies. We speak and decree healing from the crown of our heads to the soles of our feet. We speak to every physiological system and command you to function the way God created you to function. We speak to the circulatory system and command you to function. We speak to the digestive system and command you to function. We speak to the endocrine system and command you to function. We speak to the integumentary system and command you to function. We speak to the muscular system and command you to function. We speak to the nervous system and command you to function. We speak to the renal and urinary system and command you to function. We speak to the reproductive system and command you to function. We speak to the skeletal system and command you to function. All systems; you WILL function to the full capacity in which the Most High God created you! Yes, You will.

We understand that COVID-19 attacks the respiratory system, we command you to function in the name of Jesus. We speak to the lungs and command the appropriate oxygen level to flow. We speak healing of pneumonia, COPD (Chronic Obstructive Pulmonary Disease), and asthma. We speak healing. Lord, heal Your people. Breath of God, breathe over Your people. Breathe Jesus breathe! We pray that You would touch the respiratory systems of those who are in hospitals on ventilators. Lord, begin to breathe in their lungs! Breathe Jesus breathe!

We speak to the circulatory system. We command our hearts to beat the way You designed them to beat. We come against any irregular heartbeat. We come against congestive heart failure. Heart; beat normal! We come against heart attacks. Devil, you are a liar! Devil, take your hands off individuals. We pray that You, Lord would go to ICUs and cause rhythms on heart monitors to return to normal. Lord, please don't allow stress related to COVID-19 to cause any heart attacks. Lord, cause us to remain calm. We speak calmness. We will not be stressed or anxious. We cast all our cares upon You for You care for us! Thank you for caring for us!

Heal our minds Lord! We give You our minds! We choose to have the mind of Christ. We won't be conformed to the world but transformed by the renewing of our minds. (Romans 12:2

KJV) Lord cause transformation and renewal of our minds. Lord, wash our minds with Your Word. (Ephesians 5:26 KJV) We make a conscious decision to cast down imaginations, and every high thing that exalteth itself against the knowledge of God, and bringing into captivity every thought to the obedience of Christ. (2 Corinthians 10:5) We will think positive thoughts and not negative thoughts. We choose to think life and not death. We shall live and not die to declare the works of the Lord in the land of the living. (Psalm 118:7 KJV) We decree everyone attached to us will live. Life is our portion!

My Prayer, Thoughts or Revelation

WEALTH

When we think of WEALTH we think of possessing large amounts of money and material things. Wealth is also abundance. We can have an abundance of God.

Moving through this pandemic, it may not look much like wealth or abundance. Regardless of what we see, we are wealthy and walking into our season of wealth transfer. God is in this moment releasing witty and creative ideas on how to become wealthy. Yes, the wealth of the sinner is laid up for the just. (Proverbs 13.22)

As believers, it's imperative to remember we still have an inheritance. Yes, our inheritance entails abundance! There is no lack in God! There is no lack in us! We have abundance! We have increase! Just as Jesus increased in wisdom, stature, and in favor with God and man, we are increasing!

We are wealthy!

WEALTH

Father, we thank you for wealth. We declare that the wealth of the wicked is laid up for the just. (Proverbs 13: 22 KJV) We are wealthy people! We are walking in a season of increase. Lord, cause us to remember it's You that giveth us power to get wealth. (Deuteronomy 8:18 KJV) We receive Your wealth. We are walking in a wealthy season. We celebrate the wealth transfer.

We thank you that every seed of money we've sown will sprout up as a tree. Thank you, Lord, for increase of money. We decree and declare that people are going to give to us. We call people with money to come from the east, west, north, and south. We are open in this season to however wealth is coming to our hands.

We decree and declare even through this period of unemployment wealth is released. Lord, give us witty ideas on how to create multiple streams of income. We are not afraid in the season to maximize every gift and talent You have given us to walk into our wealthy season.

We decree and declare favor to get wealth. Lord, we decree You have given us favor with You as well as with man. (Luke 2:52) We decree that we are surrounded by favor like a shield. (Psalm

5:12 KJV) Favor manifests as wealth cometh! You, God is preparing a table of wealth right in front of our enemies. (Psalm 23:5 KVJ) Our enemies are going to favor us in this season! Yes, our, enemies are going to bless us in this season. We thank you for every enemy! It's a divine set-up. Lord, You're setting us up really good! We give You glory! We give You honor!

There is no lack in this season, only wealth. Lord we thank you that we are not lacking but wealthy. I've never seen the righteous forsaken nor His seed begging for bread. (Psalm 37:25 KJV) Yes, Lord we won't have to beg for anything. You're our Shepherd and we shall not want. (Psalm 23:1 KJV) There's no good thing You will withhold from us! Thank you for our season of wealth. Thank you for wealth!

My Prayer, Thoughts or Revelation

PRAYERS FOR UNCERTAIN TIMES

FEAR

FEAR: to be afraid. As the world began to hear increasing and alarming reports about coronavirus and COVID-19 a spirit of fear was released in the earth; however, we must find the strength to look fear in the face and declare: "We are not afraid and will not live in fear." God hasn't given us the spirit of fear but of power, and love, and of a sound mind. (2 Timothy 1:7 KJV)

We're not afraid of the unknown. We allow fear to dominate our world where we live in the future and miss the opportunities of today. We will take no thought for the morrow: for the morrow shall take thought for the things of itself. Sufficient unto the day is the evil thereof. The Lord will take care of us tomorrow just as He's doing today. He's the God of our today and tomorrow!

Someone's reality doesn't have to become our reality. I am not being insensitive in writing these words. The enemy will use fear of what's happening to someone else to cause us to think it's our reality. We then begin to live our lives as if we're going to become sick or die. God doesn't want us to exist in this realm of fear.

We won't fear because we will keep God in constant remembrance of His Word and His promises! God has this and us!

FEAR

Lord, You, haven't given us the spirit of fear but of power, love and a sound mind! However, we admit being afraid of the unknown. We give You our fears. We realize that our times are in Your hands. Help us to not be afraid! Lord, remind us to not take thought for the morrow, for the morrow shall take thought for the things of itself. (Matthew 6:34 KJV). We will not fear!

We will not be afraid of how were going to make it now or after COVID-19. You're the God that supplies all our needs according to your riches, in Christ Jesus. You're our source, everything else is resources for our use. We thank you that You're making a way out of no way. Yes, You are! You're a waymaker! We bless You!

Father, we won't be afraid of the "terror by night nor for the arrow that flies by day. *Nor* for the pestilence *that* walketh in darkness; *nor* for the destruction *that* wasteth at noonday. A thousand shall fall at thy side, and ten thousand at thy right hand *but* it shall not come nigh thee." (Psalm 91:5-7 KJV) It's not going to come nigh us! We're covered by The Blood! Thank you for The Blood that's covering us! Thank you Lord, for giving Your angels charge over us, to keep us in all our ways. We thank you for Your keeping power.

Father we won't fear because You are with us wherever we go. We appreciate You being with us. Thanks for never leaving us nor forsaking us. Even when some of us feel alone in this temporary pandemic, You are with us! Thank you for being with us! Yes, Immanuel (God with Us) we appreciate and adore You!

We thank you father for being a deliverer of all our fears. Lord, cause peace, calm and assuredness to come upon us as we seek You knowing that You will answer us and deliver us from all our fears. (Psalm 34:4 KJV). We thank you for delivering us! You're a great deliverer. You deliver us out of what we think is going to take us out. You're going to deliver us from the effects of COVID-19. You are Jehovah Garash, the God of the way out! Lord we're not consumed by fear. We're consumed with our exit! The snare is broken, and we are escaped. (Psalm 124:7 KJV) We escaped!

We don't fear because You're the light in midst of darkness. You are the light of our salvation; whom shall we fear? "The Lord is the strength of my life; of whom shall I be afraid!" (Psalm 27:1 KJV) We have the best illuminator! Jesus, shine Your light in our darkness. Shine Jesus, shine! Shine Jesus, Shine! Thank you, we'll see clearly as You shine!

We don't walk in fear! We don't speak fear! We speak calmness!

My Prayer, Thoughts or Revelation

FAITH

FAITH is the substance of things hoped for, the evidence of things not seen. (Hebrews 11:1 KJV) We can't see the outcome of COVID-19 but our faith says that all things are working together for our good. We can't see healing, but our faith says by Jesus' stripes we're healed. Our faith says our health is restored. We can't see our needs being met but our faith says; God will supply all our needs according to His riches in glory. (Philippians 4:19 KJV)

Faith comes by hearing and hearing by the Word of God. Our faith will increase as we hear the Word of God spoken out of our mouths. In all these things (yes, even in COVID-19) we are more than conquerors. God still knows the plans He has to prosper us and not to harm us, plans to give us hope and a future. (Jeremiah 29:11 NIV) We still say that when we pass through the waters, God will be with us, and when we pass through the rivers; they will not sweep over us. When we walk through the fire; we will not be burned, the flames will not set us ablaze (Isaiah 43:2 NIV). We still say the angel of the Lord encampeth round about us! (Psalm 34:7).

Our faith will not fail! We believe You God, period!

FAITH

Lord, we pray that You increase our faith. We choose to believe You! We understand without faith it's impossible to please You. We most certainly want to please You. Lord, all we need is faith the size of a mustard seed. (Matthew 17:20 KJV) We activate our mustard seed faith and believe You again. We walk by faith and not by sight. (2 Corinthians 5:7 KJV)

Lord, allow us to keep walking and not become distracted by what we see. Help us to see You! Help us to see those You've healed. Help us to see life and not death. Help us to see that we still have the activity of limbs. Help us to see that You're still working miracles. Lord, we shift our focus. COVID-19 will not cause us to doubt Your capability to perform miracles and perform Your promises.

Lord, please forgive us for having more faith in man's words than Your Words. It's Your Word that brings life. Your Word provides light in darkness. Your Word is a lamp unto our feet and light unto our path. (Psalm 119:105 KJV) We thank you that Your Word is forever settled in heaven and Your settled word is manifesting in every aspect of our lives. (Psalm 119:89 KJV) We believe Your Word.

Lord cause us to activate our faith by hearing Your Word. (Romans 10:17 KJV) Faith comes by hearing and hearing the Word of God. We want to hear Your Word to drown out the noise of the devil's words. Yes, help us to listen to Your Word on our electronic devices or computers. Help us to study Your Word and manifest Your Word in the earth. Lord, as we activate our faith through Your Word, we will use Your Word against the enemy. We will not only plead the blood against COVID-19, coronavirus and all related illnesses but Your Word! We decree and declare Your Word thanks be to God, who gives us the victory through our Lord Jesus Christ. (I Corinthians 15:57 KJV) Our faith in You is the indication that we are not defeated. As victory belongs to You it belongs to us! We decree faith and victory!

Lord we activate our faith by speaking to COVID-19. It will bow at the name of Jesus! You have given us the authority to speak to mountains and the mountains must move. (Mark 11:23 KJV) There's nothing impossible to You. This deadly virus looks impossible to men but with You all things are possible. (Mark 10:27 KJV) Society is causing us to think even life is impossible. The devil is a liar. We have life because we have the life giver. We will not be overcome by COVID- 19 or any other attack. Jesus, just as You overcame the world, we will overcome this. It will not conquer us. We are more than conquerors and we will conquer this pandemic! Yes, we will! Conquerors rise!

My Prayer, Thoughts or Revelation

PEACE

Peace, is calmness. It doesn't make sense but even in this pandemic we have calmness. We have the peace of God that surpasseth all man's understanding. (Philippians 4:7 KJV)

COVID-19 may look like a storm that we're going to drown in but we're not going to drown. We speak peace to this storm.

Our minds are at peace. We choose to keep our minds on the Lord. The Lord promises to keep us in perfect peace providing we keep our minds on Him! (Isaiah 26:3)

We speak; "peace be still," to our emotions. We are calm!

PEACE

We speak to COVID-19 and say; "peace be still". Lord, we thank you for the authority that we can speak peace and command things to be still. We speak to our emotions as it relates to this virus plaguing the world, and say; "peace be still". Everything that's trying to wage war against us we speak, "peace be still". Thank you, Lord, for a calmness in our environment, our spirts, our souls and the atmosphere. Thank you for peace that brings calmness. We're not anxious in this season. We have peace!

We thank you for Your peace that's calming our minds. You will keep us in prefect peace as we keep our minds stayed on You! Here's our mind Jesus, fill it with peace! Thoughts that are not pleasing to God, peace be still. Thoughts of death; peace be still. Thoughts of doom and gloom; peace be still. Our minds are peaceful.

We bless You for being the Prince of Peace! We don't have to search for peace. You're our peace and have already given us peace. Now may the Lord of peace himself give You peace always by all means. (2 Thessalonians 3:16 KJV) When our atmospheres become chaotic; we speak peace! Lord, cause us to be at peace. Yes, when we walk in let peace manifest! Peace manifest when we show up! When there's confusion, help us to be the peacemakers, for You told us in Your Word as peacemakers we shall be called the children of God. (Matthew 5:9 KJV)

Lord, we decree and declare that our sleepless nights are over. COVID-19 will not keep us up at night. We decree and declare from this night forward that we will sleep. We will sleep and sleep well! We will lay down in peace, and sleep: for You, Lord, only makest us dwell in safety. (Psalm 4:8 KJV) We can sleep because while we're sleeping, we are safe! Yes, we are!

Lord, we commit our ways to You! We want our ways to please You. When our ways please You, "You maketh even our enemies to be at peace with us!" We thank you that our enemies are going to be peaceful. (Proverbs 16:7 KJV) We will do all that we can to live in peace with everyone. (Romans 12:18 NLT) Yes, we will live in peace even with our enemies.

We appreciate Your peace that surpasses all man's understanding! (Philippians 4:7 KJV)

My Prayer, Thoughts or Revelation

CAROL J. WILLIAMS

HOPE

HOPE! HOPE is expecting good and positive results, occurrences, emotions, and outcomes despite surface appearances. Our state of mind as we walk through a global and growing pandemic must be one of hope; one that is based on the expectation of God turning COVID-19 around. Our hope is God; the God of hope! We are not hopeless. We always have hope because we have the God of Hope who's always with us!

I am reminded of one of my favorite hymns; "My hope is built on nothing less than Jesus Christ, our righteousness; I dare not trust the sweetest frame but wholly lean on Jesus name. On Christ, the solid Rock we stand; all other ground is sinking sand. All other ground is sinking sand." We won't lose hope! We have a Rock to lean on when we feel overwhelmed!

HOPE

COVID-19 will not cause us to lose our hope! We are not hopeless. We call on the God of hope. God of Hope; help Your children! Why are thou cast down, O our souls? And why art thou disquieted within us? Hope in God; for we shall yet praise Him, who is the health of our countenance, and our God (Psalm 43:5 KJV) Soul, we command you even now to hope in God!

We thank you God of hope that we're being filled with joy and peace in believing, that we may abound in hope, through the power of the Holy Ghost. (Romans 15:13 KJV) God of hope thank you for filling us! We can and will get through this because we're filled with Your hope. Our hope is in You! You're the author and finisher of our faith. (Hebrews 12:2 KJV)

We shift our hope! We don't put our hope in anyone but You! We hope in You and hope in Your Word. You are our hiding place and our shield. We hope in Your Word. We hope in Your Word, for "the word of God *is* quick, and powerful, and sharper than any two-edged sword, piercing even to the dividing asunder of soul and spirit, and of the joints and marrow, and *is* a discerner of the thoughts and intents of the heart." (Hebrews 4:12) We hope in

Your Word that's quick. Yes, quick enough to even turn COVID-19 around. We hope in Your quick word. Lord, manifest Your quick word in the Earth.

We choose to hope in You because You're our confidence!

My Prayer, Thoughts or Revelation

PRAYERS FOR UNCERTAIN TIMES

STRENGTH

Strength, the state of being strong. There are times where we just don't feel like being strong. If we tell the truth everything related to the strain of coronavirus that began wreaking havoc in late 2019 is one of those times. God is our strength. The Lord gives power to the weak, and to those who have no might; He increases strength.

Lord, because of Your strength we can do anything!

STRENGTH

Lord, we thank you for strength! You are our strength. Lord, we admit there are times where we feel weak; however, it's when we're weak that's when we say; "we are strong." We admit we're only strong because of You. Our truth is COVID-19 causes us to feel that our strength is being depleted. We thank you that as You strengthen us, You keep us on our feet. You are the God who's able to keep us from falling.

The enemy wants to make us think that we no longer can do certain things because of a worldwide virus. The devil is a liar and the father of lies! We can and will do all things through Christ who gives us strength. During this pandemic give us the strength to embrace new ideas and new opportunities. Lord, cause us even in the presence of this virus attacking bodies to advance the Kingdom to bring You Glory! We only want to bring You Glory! We can and will succeed! Yes, we will! We will not fail! We will and can function despite COVID-19! Yes, we can!

We speak to those who are weary! We won't be weary in doing well in waiting upon the Lord. (2 Thessalonians 3:13 KJV) Our flesh and our hearts may fail, but God is the strength of our hearts and our portion forever. (Psalm 73:26 KJV)

Lord we will wait on You and be of good courage knowing that You're going to strengthen our hearts. Strengthen our hearts Lord! We embrace Your strength. (Psalm 27:14 KJV) Lord, because You are strengthening us, our wait will no longer be a weight. We don't know when You're going to answer our prayers concerning turning things around and shattering the presence of every attack born out of this strain of the coronavirus but we wait. Strengthen our wait! Thank you, Jesus!

We thank you for Your strength to continue the fight. We won't take flight because we have strength to fight. Lord give us strength and teach our hands how to war. We're strengthened for the fight. We thank you as we fight; we win! We give You praise! (Psalm 144:1 KJV)

My Prayer, Thoughts or Revelation

LOVE

The best definition of LOVE is found in First Corinthians 13:1-8 (KJV). Lord, let love reign now, even more.

> "Though I speak with the tongues of men and of angels, and have not charity, I am become as sounding brass, or a tinkling cymbal.
>
> ² And though I have the gift of prophecy, and understand all mysteries, and all knowledge; and though I have all faith, so that I could remove mountains, and have not charity, I am nothing.
>
> ³ And though I bestow all my goods to feed the poor, and though I give my body to be burned, and have not charity, it profiteth me nothing.
>
> ⁴ Charity suffereth long, and is kind; charity envieth not; charity vaunteth not itself, is not puffed up,

⁵ Doth not behave itself unseemly, seeketh not her own, is not easily provoked, thinketh no evil;

⁶ Rejoiceth not in iniquity, but rejoiceth in the truth;

⁷ Beareth all things, believeth all things, hopeth all things, endureth all things.

⁸ Charity never faileth: but whether there be prophecies, they shall fail; whether there be tongues, they shall cease; whether there be knowledge, it shall vanish away."

LOVE

For You so love the world that You gave Your only begotten son that whosoever believeth in him shouldn't perish but have everlasting life. (John 3:16) There's no greater love than this, than to lay down one's life for his friend. (John 15:13 KJV) Jesus we thank you for Your love. Thank you for loving us unconditionally.

We ask You father to forgive us for not allowing our love to be reciprocal. We apologize for not loving You with all our heart, and with all our soul, and with all our strength, and with all our mind. (Luke 10:27 KJV) We command our entire being from this day forth to love You.

Lord, forgive us for not demonstrating true love. Every time we feel as if we can't endure anything, remind us, love suffers long. Every time we're unkind to people, remind us that love is kind. Every time we think of ourselves more highly than we ought to, remind us love is not puffed up. Lord, remind us true love never fails. (1 Corinthians 13:4-8 KJV)

Lord, remind us that we display our love by doing what you have asked us to do. Help us to obey You. Lord forgive us for not obeying You. Even in the midst of COVID-19 You've been trying to get our attention. You've told us to increase our prayer time. You've told us to increase our Word study. You've told us to fast. You've told us to turn the TV off. You've told us to decrease social media usage. We continued to be disobedient; please forgive us. Lord, we give You another, yes, we will obey. We make a conscious decision to submit to Your will, purpose, and plan for our lives. As we love You, Your will be done! (Matthew 6:10 KJV)

Lord, help us love ourselves. We can't love our neighbors until we begin to love ourselves. Our neighbors during this time need our love. Lord, help us to see ourselves as You see us. We appreciate You seeing us fearfully and wonderfully made in Your image. (Genesis 1:27) Remind us that everything You created was good. Yes, we're good! You loved us so much that You know the thoughts that You think towards us, thoughts of peace, and not of evil, to give us an expected end. (Jeremiah 29:11 KJV) We will love ourselves by taking care of the body You have loaned us. Lord, help us to do right by our bodies. We will love ourselves.

During this time of COVID-19 we will love our neighbors. We will love all individuals. We will love our neighbors who have done us wrong. We will love our neighbors who've said all manner of evil against us falsely for Your sake. We choose to love them. We know that we are blessed according to Your Word when we do so. (Matthew 5:11 KJV). We will love our enemies and bless those that curse us. We will show our love by blessing our neighbors and even our enemies. We will love our neighbors.

We love and appreciate You for being such an awesome and amazing God. We will love You, love ourselves, and love our neighbors.

My Prayer, Thoughts or Revelation

HUMILITY

HUMILITY is the quality of being HUMBLE or not prideful. We must humble ourselves under the mighty hand of God, that He may exalt us in due time. Let's get under His hand and not stay above His hand. Let's allow God to be exalted in COVID-19 and in all things.

As we humble ourselves, let's be okay with asking for assistance when needed and receiving assistance. Let's not allow pride to cause us to go lacking. The Lord is our provider and uses people to meet needs. Let's get under the hand of God and stay there.

HUMILITY

Father, we thank you for being the humble Lamb. As we want to always reflect Your character, help us be humble. Lord, we humble ourselves under Your hand knowing in due season You will exalt us! We humble under Your hand and not above Your hand. Please forgive us for attempting to be the leader with the expectation that You will follow. Lord, You lead us and we will follow.

We understand our following is when we can walk in divinely-ordered steps. The steps of a good man are ordered by the Lord. Order our steps Jesus. Lord, it's You that guides the humble in what is right and teaches us Your way. (Psalm 25:9 KJV) We submit to Your will! We no longer want our way. We want You and Your way.

We come against the spirit of pride as pride comes before a fall. We don't want to fall; so we denounce pride in the name of Jesus! We will not be prideful. Lord, help us during COVID-19 to let go of pride. Help us to be transparent when we need something. Help us Lord, to be okay with reaching out for help. Help us kill pride before it kills us! Jesus, we need You to help us!

Lord arise and be exalted! We will no longer be exalted! You reign Jesus. We dethrone ourselves and put You back on the throne. We take a seat! You are exalted above all gods – especially the god of self! As You are exalted, we exalt You and not ourselves. We exalt You God! God be thou exalted! We want You to take Your rightful place in our lives.

Lord, we thank you for a great inheritance that You've already given us; however, remind us it's the meek who will inherit the earth. Lord, help us humble ourselves so we won't forfeit our inheritance. We humble ourselves!

Lord, help us to realize the healing of our land is based on our ability to humble ourselves. If Your people which are called by Your name, shall humble ourselves, and pray, and seek Your face, and turn from our wicked ways; then will You hear from heaven, and will forgive our sins, and will heal our land. (2 Chronicles 7:14 KJV) Help us understand the importance of our humility as we call on Your name to see our land healed!

Lord, as we humble ourselves, we relinquish our control!

We allow You to have complete control!

My Prayer, Thoughts or Revelation

GRIEF

GRIEF is real! Grief is the normal reaction to any type of loss. Whether we want to admit it; we all have experienced loss related to the coronavirus. It's okay to feel what you feel.

It's imperative to give yourself permission, time and space to grieve. Allow yourself to experience the normal emotions that come with grieving – anger, sadness, confusion, uncertainty. And know that It's okay for men and women to cry. Jesus wept! Jesus does not discount your tears; nor does He think your tears represent a lack of faith. He knows that you need a season of comfort, and He reminds us that we are never without comfort because He is the Comforter.

The Lord will provide strength to us as we grieve. He is our strength and will never leave us. We're not alone. God is with us during our tears and pain. God is greater than the pain. Trust Him with your grief.

GRIEF

At the time this book was written, there were over 100,000 deceased individuals globally related to COVID-19 and complications. Father, we lift up every grieving family. We pray You send Your comfort and strength. You can send comfort and strength because that is who You are. Father strengthen them and comfort them.

We pray that each grieving family would allow themselves to grieve and be okay with leaning into grief. Allow them to identify their true emotions, deal with them, and give them over to You so that healing can begin.

Lord, let them know that it's okay to cry and that You understand their tears. You, Father, have their tears in a precious bottle. Jesus, You wept when receiving the news of Lazarus' death, which is a great example for them to be okay with crying. (John 11:35 KJV) You said in Your Word, blessed are they that mourn for they shall be comforted. (Matthew 5:4 KJV) As grieving families mourn remind them, they are blessed and comforted.

Lord, we pray for grieving families who now are afraid of the unknown. We pray that You wonderfully let them to know that

You have them in the palm of Your hand. You have them! Wrap Your mighty and comforting arms around them.

Lord, we pray You would allow them to reach out for help and support. Please Lord, allow them to know that they're not alone. Lord, You are with them and allow them to know that others are with them. Allow them to know it's okay to pray and get professional help. Lord, allow them to embrace support.

Lord, we pray that grieving families would continue to live and find ways to honor and celebrate their loved one's memory and their legacy.

Lord, COVID-19 has caused all of us to experience grief, the normal and natural emotion to any type of loss. We pray for the millions of people who are now unemployed because of this devastating virus. We pray You provide them Your strength and comfort. We pray for resources. We pray Lord they would understand anew that You are their source. We pray for all grieving individuals throughout the land.

Lord, when we feel like we are about to drown in our tears and pain leads to the dry shore, we won't drown in grief. When our hearts are overwhelmed lead us to the rock that's higher than we are. You're our rock and sure foundation. (Psalm 61:2 KJV) You got us!

We will not die! We won't be afraid we're going to die because we've lost family members to this virus. We will live to see the goodness of You in our land. There's still goodness in our land. (Psalm 27: 13 KJV). Lord, give us the strength to live in and embrace the newness you are birthing through this pandemic. We speak life! We decree life! We find the strength to embrace life.

As we grieve, grief won't become our identity. We will identify with You and who You've called us to be while we experience a wide range of emotions. Yes, we still are fearfully and wonderfully made. (Psalm 139:14 KJV) We still are above only and not beneath. (Deuteronomy 28:13 KJV) We still are accepted by You! (Eph 1:6 KJV) Yes, we are!

We give You praise, Glory and honor because You are comforting us and keeping us as we grieve!

My Prayer, Thoughts or Revelation

Thank you so much for reading Christ Optimizes Victory In Desolation.

I pray the book has been a blessing to you. Please spread these words of hope and assurance.

Also, please take a moment to let me know how these words impacted you. I would greatly appreciate it.

You can contact me for speaking engagements or further information by email or by visiting the website for ICare Solutions.

www.icaresolutions.website
ChristOptimizesVictory@outlook.com
Continual Blessings,
Carol Williams

ABOUT THE AUTHOR

Elder Carol J. Williams is founder of I Care Solutions a community-based organization formed to improve the lives of the broken, outcasts and disenfranchised. She is an RN, author of the books Writing While Surviving 30-Day Journal, *A Seed For A Day-God's Word Producing Productivity*, *Beyond The Pretty Dress-Women Serving Powerfully Beyond Church Walls* (Contributing Author) *Motivate Me Magazine*(Contributing Covenant Writer), and Grief Recovery Specialist Certified by Grief Recovery Method Institute, Ministry leader, Intercessor and (former) radio talk show host, accomplishments include, serving as Director of Education for HIV/AIDS Awareness program, Founder and President of Jewels Causing Change for Christ Women's Ministry.

www.ingramcontent.com/pod-product-compliance
Lightning Source LLC
Chambersburg PA
CBHW052111070526
44584CB00017B/2433